Your Amazing Itty Bitty Business Dating Book

15 Steps to Finding and Working With the Right People for Your Business

If you're a solopreneur or just starting a new business, navigating the process of hiring employees and acquiring other collaborative relationships might be unfamiliar to you. However, you do have experience with, both friends and romantic relationships. Think of it like dating – meeting someone, getting to know them, trusting them, and potentially parting ways in the future.

Barbara Robins is passionate about high-performance transformation. In her book, she will help you navigate your business dating journey. Barbara provides tools necessary to build and maintain the business collaborations that contribute to your company's success - employees, contractors, partnerships, consultants, and others.

By reading this book you will:

- Know simple strategies for successfully finding people with whom you can work
- Understand how to identify and address challenging situations
- Recognize the importance of integrity, respect, and cooperation in all your communications
- And so much more!

Ready to seek out and maintain superior business alliances, pick up a copy of this must-read Itty Bitty™ book today!

Your Amazing
Itty Bitty™
Business Dating
Book

*15 Steps to Finding and Working With the
Right People for Your Business*

Barbara Robins

Published by Itty Bitty™ Publishing
A subsidiary of Unlimited Possibilities, Inc.

Copyright © 2024 **Barbara Robins**

Printed in the United States of America.

Itty Bitty Publishing
311 Main Street, Suite E
El Segundo, CA 90245
(310) 640-8885

ISBN: 978-1-7322946-1-5

Dedication

In the grad school of life, I believe that in one way or another, most of the circumstances and people I have crossed paths with have contributed to conceiving and birthing this book. So, I dedicate it to all those who are threads in the tapestry that is my life.

Specifically, my experiences at CEO Space Inc. forums were the major accelerator behind the idea for this book. I am grateful to faculty member Dr. David Gruder who, perhaps unknowingly, prompted me to write it. Thank you, Dr. Gruder.

I want to thank Mike Jimenez and Katie Forbes for listening to me "talk the book" in its beginning stages and for giving me editorial notes. Sharon Lewis, an HR manager at Paychex, Inc. was so helpful in reviewing the manuscript to be sure I wasn't making any HR-related mistakes. Katie Forbes, an additional huge thank you, my friend, for reviewing the book a second time when it was near completion, and also for your yoga teacher-HR professional mashup of wisdom during your second round of notes.

My sincere thanks also go to Ellen Kratka, Tahira Aziz, Libbe Halevy, and Carol Wachniak, whose friendship and professional collaboration in so many ways over so many years brings tears to my eyes. I am beyond thankful and grateful for your unconditional love, wisdom, and awesome energy work.

Suzy Prudden, your idea for Itty Bitty Publishing was so perfect. For two years this book sat in my brain gathering dust as the thought of writing a 150-page book was too daunting when I had only a one-paragraph idea. You know your impact on my life. Thank you.

And lastly, my heartfelt thanks to the 1950s yellow kitchen chair that was part of my life for over 50 years. That chair was the catalyst that awakened my curiosity.

You see, I had just sharpened a pencil and the chair was right there. I was compelled to poke a hole in the cushion with the pencil. The puncturing sound and physical sensation of the pencil point through the vinyl seat cushion was mesmerizing (think bubble wrap). I kept poking holes in the seat cushion until my mother caught me. I was four years old.

The intensity of her anger seemed a little much as I wasn't just poking random holes in the cushion. I had thought this through and was making a flower. An improvement to the looks of the chair, right?

 Nevertheless, the chair with my unfinished design that looked like a lollipop was banished to the basement where it stayed for 40 years, reminding me of the shame I was supposed to feel every time I saw it.

We didn't know it at the time, but I've been poking at things ever since. My fascination with breaking barriers and out-of-the-box thinking has served me well ever since.

For more valuable information about business dating, please visit our Itty Bitty website:

www.ittybittypublishing.com

Or visit Barbara Robins' website:

https://happybusinessresults.com

Table of Contents

Introduction

This book transforms the mystery of business vetting into simple concepts you can relate to and have probably experienced. The goal is to make finding and working with people easier and more successful in the long run.

If you are a solopreneur or starting your first business, you probably don't have prior experience hiring people. In addition, you probably don't have a human relations department to handle hiring. However, you do have experience with relationships, both friendships and romantic ones. You understand how it feels to meet, get to know, open yourself to trusting people, and perhaps down the line disengage or break up with them.

When you finish reading this book you will:

- Know simple strategies for successfully finding people with whom you can work
- Understand how to identify and address challenging situations
- Recognize the importance of integrity, respect and cooperation in all your communications

And now a word from Brad Szollose, author, serial entrepreneur, business advisor, and host of Awakened Nation podcast®, on how this book will impact your business relationships.

"I distinctly remember meeting Barbara Robins in Chicago almost a decade ago. I was speaking at a Mind Capture Boot Camp for Tony Rubleski. There, in the lobby, deeply embedded in the couches, Barbara was helping a friend with her phone. I stepped in to help and we all struck up a conversation.

"As a former C-level executive of a publicly traded company, I have learned the secret to my own success: soft skills. A study was released a few years ago that confirmed it all—soft skills are the key to success in business and life.

"Barbara's enthusiasm and understanding of human relationships are apparent within the pages of *Your Amazing Itty Bitty™ Business Dating Book.* Get a pen and paper and some highlighters, because she has broken down the steps to frictionless work and life. I have had dozens of issues with business partners, narcissists, and 'hard to work with' clients through the years. I wish I had this book 35 years ago; it could have saved me a lot of wasted energy and time.

"It's time to stop struggling. You now have the secret to success in your hand. I tip my hat to Barbara Robins. Thank you for putting this masterwork in our hands."

Step 1
Mirror, Mirror on the Wall

*"Knowing yourself is the beginning
of all wisdom."*
~ *Aristotle*

1. Before you start your search for the right people (both partnerships and employees), begin by looking at your competencies, strengths, weaknesses, and interpersonal attributes.
2. Oil and water don't mix, so understanding yourself and what matters to you will help you select people you can work with who will add value to your business.
3. Learn to recognize the signals your gut and heart send you. They help you make better decisions.

Resources to Illuminate Who You Are [1]

- **Myers-Briggs Personality Test**
  Identify how you perceive the world and make decisions. The results of this test provide insight into how your personality type is best suited for success in terms of careers, communication, etc. M-B is also a great screening and interviewing tool.
- **Human Design**
  Each person's Human Design chart is uniquely individual and demonstrates strategy and authority. If applied correctly, this information results in good decision-making.
- **Straight Talk**
  Learn your communication style and gain insight into how you can improve interactions with others. Create a team account to improve team communication.
- **CliftonStrengths Assessment**
  Learn the 34 ways to describe what you naturally do best.
- **Illuminating the Deeper You**
  This is an exercise that uncovers critical choices and experiences that have impacted your life. Follow up with a complimentary 30-minute Activation of Possibility consultation.

---

[1] Link for resources: http://resources.bizdating.biz

Step 2
Howling at the Moon

When you can't find the right person to work with, you may feel like howling at the moon in frustration or desperation.

Possible reasons the right person hasn't shown up:

1. You are not in alignment with your highest and best outcome.
2. Your desired outcome is designed to fulfill your inner lust or illusions.
3. You are not taking inspired action.
4. You have unconscious negative feelings about people who do that type of work.
5. You have a conscious and/or unconscious belief that you'll never find the right person for the job.
6. You think you know better than anyone else how to find that right person.
7. You think you can do the job better than anyone else, so you don't want to hand it over to anyone.

Things to Do Instead of Howling at the Moon

- Relax, you are loved and watched over. Let this sink in: author and priest Brennan Manning said, "I am now utterly convinced that on judgment day, the Lord Jesus will ask one question and only one question. "Did you believe that I loved you?"
- Breathe deeply and allow yourself to trust that *all that is* knows what your highest and best outcomes are and is actually conspiring for you to succeed.
- Get 100% clear and certain with your head and heart agreeing about your true desires for this business endeavor or project, and why you want it.
- Create a Strategic Attraction Plan.[1]
- Go about business as usual, knowing that your next inspired action step will come to mind. (See Step 4, Dancing With the Universe.)
- For numbers 4, 5, and/or 6 on the prior page, schedule sessions with an energy optimizer to uncover and resolve your conscious or unconscious beliefs and resistances. [2]

---

[1] Links for resources: http://resources.bizdating.biz
[2] Links for resources: http://resources.bizdating.biz

Step 3
Business Crushes

In your personal life, you know you have a crush on someone when you are very attracted to them but know very little about them. The same can happen with potential business relationships.

1. Committing to a collaboration with stars in your eyes can derail your business and/or set you back in time and money.
2. At first look, you might think someone is a good candidate for collaboration, but you could be infatuated with what appears to be business savvy or a captivating personality.
3. Regaining calm objectivity can be challenging when you're excited about someone. Ask yourself, "Is this person a good fit for me and my business endeavor?"
4. Carefully read the following chapters for steps on how to avoid entanglement with someone who isn't qualified for your project and/or doesn't mesh well with other team members.

Types of Biz Crushes

- The admiration crush: When you idolize a person (like a celebrity or teacher you think is awesome).
- The passing crush: It's human nature to be attracted to other people. This new person may seem new and exciting, and they probably are, but that doesn't mean you should work with them.

How You Feel

- Do you feel "less than" around this person?
- Do you feel they are "better than" you? [1]
- When you consider working with this person do you feel an excited *yes* in your head or a calm, quiet *yes* in your gut?
- Do you feel you are a better you when working with this person?
- Notice if you feel free to focus on your area of expertise or if you often find yourself double-checking their work.
- Do you have that sense where together you create bigger and better results than you could produce individually?

---

[1] If you feel less than a potential collaborator or that they are better than you, schedule some sessions with an energy optimizer or life coach to resolve this as those are self-esteem issues that will cloud your decision-making ability.

Step 4
Dancing With the Universe

Music has a rhythm and pace. When you dance freely, you're in sync with the rhythm of the music. Life has a rhythm and pace, too.

1. When you're in alignment with the universe (God, or *all that is,* or whatever term you prefer), life flows naturally.
2. When you're in sync with the rhythm of life, people and events move your projects forward efficiently and effectively.
3. When you dance in sync with the universe you are calm and stress-free.
4. When you slow dance with a partner, only one person leads. Guess what? Every day all day you are dancing with the universe and the universe always leads.

Your Dance Partner and Choreographer

- In addition to being your dance partner, the universe is also a choreographer where everyone is part of a never-ending group dance.
- When you aren't enjoying the dance, reread Step 2, "Howling at the Moon."
- Sometimes when you're not enjoying the dance of life there is something for you to learn.
    - You may need to take some time to relax.
    - You may need to look at the situation differently.
    - This may be an opportunity to take what seems like a step back, but it's actually propelling you forward.
- Dancing with the Universe is also about switching partners. When a collaboration comes to the end of its beneficial purpose the universe always gives you a clear signal that it's time to switch partners, and then points the way.

Step 5
First Business Date

After you "swipe right" (choose yes) over the qualifications of a potential collaborator (employee, independent contractor, coach, etc.), it is time to determine their compatibility with your organization.

1. The first, second, and third business dates are more like phases that occur over a period of days or weeks.
2. The fastest and easiest way I know to learn the basics of someone's personality and character is via assessment tools. My favorite tools are on the next page.
3. In terms of human relationships, the more you learn about someone's character, the better it will be for your business.
4. Be sure you feel a strong *yes* before proceeding to the next step. If you have doubts, hold off.
5. By consistently having clarity and certainty, you will more often make good decisions instead of learning lessons.

My Favorite Resources for Understanding People[1]

- **Myers-Briggs Type Indicator®
  (MBTI®).** Identify how you perceive the
  world and make decisions. The results of
  this test provide insight into how your
  personality type is best suited for success
  in terms of careers, communication, etc.
  M-B is also a great screening and
  interviewing tool.
- **Human Design (BodyGraph).** Using
  birth information, your Human Design
  chart is uniquely individual, your best
  decision-making strategy, and how to
  live as your true self.
- **HBDI® assessment**. This is a powerful
  tool that defines and describes one's
  communication, decision-making, and
  problem-solving style.
- ***The Secret Language of Relationships.***
  This astrology-based book shows how
  your strengths and weaknesses emerge in
  collaboration with others.
- **A trusted intuitive**. An intuitive person
  you trust may be able to sense what
  collaborating with someone will be like
  for you.

---

[1] Link for resources: http://resources.bizdating.biz

Step 6
Second Business Date

So, the first meeting went well. There was good rapport between you and a good level of comfort. Now it's time to see if their ideas and style are in sync with your business philosophy.

1. Some people mistakenly hire based on qualifications alone, not knowing whether they get along, or have a clear understanding of project/job objectives, or even if they share your principles.
2. Be sure you agree on business philosophy. The better aligned your business styles, the more effective and efficient your working relationship will be.
3. Have your prospective collaborator review your company code of honor,[1] which represents your work and relationship ethics.
4. Check in with your trusted advisor.

[1] Link for resources: http://resources.bizdating.biz

Drilling Down on Alignment

- **Goals.** Be sure to discuss your goals in detail. Is the interviewee in alignment with them?
- **Code of honor.** When your prospective collaborator understands and agrees with your business philosophy, your collaboration should be on firm ground. See the online resources page for more details on how to write a code of honor.
- **Your heart as trusted advisor.** Your mind may advise you about the prospective collaborator based on ego and fear, but there is no ego or fear in your heart.
- **Other trusted advisor.** This is someone you know whose assessments and decisions are accurate most of the time. To double-check my own intuitive knowing I usually consult two or three people.
- If you aren't sure about your heart's guidance, or you aren't sure you trust your advisor's advice, see the online resource page for a link to the "Illuminating the Deeper You" exercise.

Step 7
Try Before You Buy

In personal relationships buying a plant together, making plans, or going on a little adventure together can bring out both communication strengths and challenges. It's the same in business collaborations.

1. If you can, work on a small or sample project with your prospective collaborator before committing to someone who requires a large investment of time and money.
    a. This gives both of you the opportunity to see if you work well together.
    b. It's empowering for both of you, especially as they deserve to see if they like working with you.
2. Even when it seems you and your prospective collaborator's business philosophy and project objectives are in sync, when you actually work together you may discover critical problems that make working together impossible.

Try Before You Buy

- If you have a large project, break it down into small components. Have the prospective collaborator work on one of them. For example, if you need help writing a book, ask the collaborator to help with one chapter before committing to their help with the entire book.
- You can also select a small project to see how the collaborator handles it.
- Another "try before you buy" type of arrangement is to agree on working together for a trial period. At the end of the trial, evaluate how it's going and whether it should continue.
- When hiring an assistant, I always explain that hiring isn't marriage, it's "business dating." So, we spend a few months working together, and at any time either party can decide not to continue. It's a no-fault breakup, otherwise known as a trial period.
- After 90 days, I sit down with this new assistant/collaborator and we review each other. If things are working out well, I give them a little salary bump or a small gift.

Step 8
Sealing the Deal

By now, both of you feel confident that you can work together. You know with certainty there is mutual compatibility in style and business philosophy.

To establish commitment, prepare documents of agreement that outline your objectives and standards of operation. Think of this as a prenuptial agreement.

Here are some types of documents to seal the deal:

1. Partnership or incorporation agreements
2. Job or project description
3. Business code of honor
4. Work-for-hire agreement
5. "Business baby" agreement (See Step 9)
6. Escape clause (Step 12)
7. Policy for handling conflict resolution

More Tips to Seal the Deal

- Never make decisions or choices when you feel desperate or unsure of yourself.
- Make decisions only when you feel clear and certain.
- Work with people who bring out the best in you.
- Don't work with someone if you feel "less than" or diminished in some way when interacting with them.
- If someone does creative work for you such as writing, graphic design, website development, product design, etc., be sure they sign a work-for-hire agreement.[1]
- If you feel uncertain in any way about working with this person, do not seal the deal.

---

[1] Link for resources: http://resources.bizdating.biz

Step 9
Business Babies

Business babies are the result of your creative ideas or creative collaboration with someone else. Before that baby is birthed it is vital to define your roles in taking care of the baby, including custody if there is a business divorce or you dissolve the business.

Types of business babies:

1. You and your partner birthed a business. This business itself is the baby.
2. You and another person have birthed a product in which you are both part owners.
3. You and another person have birthed a product where you have sole ownership.
4. You, alone, have birthed a business or product where you are the sole owner.

Things to Consider

- If a company is sold or goes bankrupt and you have trademarks, copyrights, and patents, who will get ownership?
- If someone is doing creative work for you or your company, is there a signed work-for-hire agreement?
- If a work-for-hire agreement is not in place, the artist/creator owns the work and can stop you from using it even if it is significant or inherent to your brand.

Step 10
Button Pushers

When you think about your significant relation-ships—parents, roommates, spouses, partners, employers, co-workers, and employees—you know that conflict is inevitable. Let's look at ways to defuse those situations.

1. Some people are in your life to facilitate your growth. Pushing your buttons reveals feelings or issues you have yet to resolve for yourself.
2. The best response to these button pushers, (though uncomfortable at first) is: "Thank you for being my teacher," as this awareness will help you grow.
3. When you experience conflict with someone, the root of the problem often is deeper than you think. Journal or meditate, asking yourself, "What is underneath this?"
4. In every conversation, business and personal, there's a pursuer and a receiver (leader and follower). That dynamic can change by the minute.
5. The best leaders listen more than they talk. Learn to listen and listen to learn.

Things to Consider When Your Buttons Are Pushed

- Learning and remembering to thank someone for being a teacher and asking, "What's underneath this?" takes a lot of practice. To get to the root of a problem quickly and easily, work with an energy optimizer to address unconscious, unresolved triggers.
- Always look at yourself first to resolve unconscious triggers. Then try to better understand the person who triggered you. Just because they see things differently doesn't make them wrong. For example, an accountant and a salesperson can be at odds over the way money is allocated in the business. Neither one is wrong.
- Acknowledge the value and contribution of the button pusher. Look at things from their perspective. This may actually change your position about what irritated you.
- Parts of a person's personality are hardwired and will always be like that. Develop an understanding of other people's personalities and working styles.[1]

---

[1] Link for resources: http://resources.bizdating.biz

Step 11
We Can Work It Out

When things go poorly between you and anyone you work with, you might start to think about ending things, getting a "business divorce." Don't despair; there are ways to resolve the situation or separate amicably.

1. Conflict resolution can be scary and challenging but know with certainty that unresolved interpersonal problems can contribute to a toxic workplace.
2. The good news is that two parties can resolve disagreements if they're both willing and have good communication skills. See Listener/Speaker guide on the resources page: http://resources.bizdating.biz
3. Is it me or is it them? See Step 10, "Button Pushers."
4. You have to be emotionally neutral in order to have a truly productive conversation.
5. Discuss the company code of honor with participants. That may be all you need to resolve your conflict.

How to Work It Out

- When you're emotionally neutral, you'll be able to figure out if talking to the other side will be productive.
- Ask yourself:
  - Is what I have to say true?
  - Is it fair?
  - Will it build goodwill and better relationships?
  - Will it be beneficial to all concerned?
- Ask them, "Are you willing to work together to find a solution so we're both happy?" If they say yes, great! If they say no, it may be time to bring it to HR or to discharge one or more parties.
- Conflict resolution first steps
  - **Cooling off.** Give yourself a few days to see if the dissonance goes away.
  - **Still hot, part 1.** Talk to a trusted advisor to see if you can resolve the problem on your own.
  - **Still hot, part 2.** Meet with the other side to discuss resolving the problem together.

Step 12
The Escape Clause

In relationships, there may come a time when the affiliation is no longer working well. The business isn't thriving, someone isn't pulling their weight, etc., and divorce is inevitable. The existence of an escape clause will help make a separation less difficult.

1. Relationships of all kinds are learning experiences or stepping-stones. When they've run their course, it's time to cut ties and set yourself and them free.
2. An escape clause is part of your sealing the deal agreement. (See Step 8, "Sealing the Deal.")
3. What criteria do you use to determine if the relationship needs to end? Your written business agreement should clearly delineate the steps to take.
4. Also covered is severance pay, if any, and business baby ownership.

A New Perspective

- People come into your life for a reason, a season, or a lifetime. If it's for a reason or a season, how can you be mad that it's not for a lifetime?
- When it's time for people to part ways, look at it as "no-fault." It is simply *all that is* saying, "New dance, switch partners."
- No hard feelings, no ill will. Everyone is free to branch out and go down that next fork in the road.
- You've imploded in your relationship together because you both know on some level that it's time for a change.
- Also, let go of resentments. The more you hold on to resentments or any negative feelings about the person or breakup, the more you close yourself off to new and better opportunities for your business.
- Everything happens for a reason and that reason is to support you. Really!
- Thank the person and thank *all that is* for the collaboration you had, as well as what brought you to this place of releasing that collaboration so you can both move forward into your next chapter.

Step 13
Mourning to Move Forward

When you have the same difficulties with several people that you work with, it could mean you have some unfinished business from past relationships.

1. If your business is not progressing and succeeding to its full potential, you may unconsciously be carrying some sadness or grief over past collaborations that ended poorly.
2. This sadness, grief, anger, etc. may be from personal or business relationships.
3. It's important to have total mental and emotional closure about past relation-ships so nothing from the past weighs you down from going forward.
4. Inner work and introspection are called for to find the roots of your sadness, grief, anger, etc.

Action Items

- Journal or meditate. Ask yourself, "What unconscious wounds am I holding on to?"
- The sadness, anger, or other feelings or beliefs you have can have their roots in childhood experiences, so you might not easily recognize them from a specific business relationship.
- Sometimes mourning shows up as self-sabotage or lack of self-confidence. Go back and read Step 1, "Mirror, Mirror on the Wall" again.
- Working with a life coach and/or quantum energy optimizer can help you pinpoint and resolve your unconscious feelings and beliefs that are holding you in a state of mourning.
- Once you have resolved the energetic roots of the wound you will attract different types of people who are better suited for this new phase of your life.

Step 14
Oops! I Did It Again

Are you finding that some of your collaborations are dysfunctional in the same way, like marrying the same type of person two or three times? To break the pattern, you have to address the roots of the problem.

1. This repeated unconscious working with the "same" person puts a strain on your business. Productivity suffers and ultimately the emotional health of everyone in the business.
2. Don't beat yourself up about this. There are no mistakes, just lessons to be learned.
3. Your unconscious vibrates your problem, so you attract people who are like mirrors that reveal your wounds. This happens for your growth. And you thought your endeavor was just to make awesome widgets. Surprise! Growing and healing wounds is always a part of the universe's plan.
4. Once you resolve the vibrational roots of your wound, you will attract someone who more positively resonates with you.

Do the Work, It's Worth It!

- Being afraid to make a mistake leads you to repeat your prior choices. Think of it this way—are you hesitant to order a different flavor of ice cream than your usual? If so, you might have trouble making the right decision on bigger things.
- Do you ever think, "Eh, leave well enough alone?" If so, you are sabotaging your success![1]
- Doing the internal work will help to find the reason you keep repeatedly working with the "same" person.
- Journal or meditate on, "What am I to learn from this?"
- Working with a life coach and quantum energy optimizer can help you get to the root of why you keep attracting the "same" person.

---

[1] Link for resources: http://resources.bizdating.biz

Step 15
Ménage à Trois

People issues are common in business. If you are embroiled in conflict with a collaborator that you can't seem to resolve on your own, you need to bring in a third party.

1. The purpose of this ménage à trois (threesome) is to bring about an effective solution with the assistance of someone who is objective and skilled with conflict resolution.
2. You'll either work out your problem, find a strategy to minimize what triggers you, or decide to end the collaboration.
3. The third party can mediate, bring accountability to the situation, or simply act as a witness.
4. You can see the third party together, alone, or a combination of both.

It's either Internal or External or a Combo

- **Internal** may mean the source of the conflict is in you. Or it may mean the way to the solution comes from inside your company.
- **External** may mean the source of the conflict comes from outside of you – another person, situation or work rule that you have no control over.
- **Internal ménage à trois.** Talk with a trusted advisor employed in your company. They may be able to help you figure out if the source of the conflict can be resolved by doing inner work on yourself, or if it involves another person or work rule.
- **External ménage à trois.** Talk privately to one of your trusted personal advisors. This can be a friend, business coach, or quantum energy optimizer.
- **Business ménage à trois.** Contact Barbara Robins to learn how a quantum energy optimization business ménage à trois may be right for your situation. https://www.happybusinessresults.com/

You've finished. Before you go …

Share/post that you finished this book.

Please star rate this book.

Reviews are solid gold to writers. Please take a few minutes to give us some itty bitty feedback.

ABOUT THE AUTHOR

With a passion for high-performance transformation, Barbara Robins has been at the forefront of innovative healing services and training since 2001. She empowers entrepreneurs, professional athletes, healers, and artists to shatter self-imposed limitations and exceed their expectations. As a master energy optimizer and trainer, Barbara guides her clients from competence to mastery in both business and personal realms, fostering calm, clarity, and certainty.

Over the past two decades, Barbara has cultivated an international practice, serving clients and students in more than 50 countries. Her advanced distant energy healing methods have accelerated transformations worldwide.

Highlights of her success include:

- Transforming a world-class athlete's career, helping them win their first Olympic gold medal in just seven weeks.
- Resolving persistent workplace interpersonal stresses for one of Oprah Winfrey's executive producers by shifting the production staff's energy.

A pioneer of 21st-century healing, Barbara offers her proprietary Energy Optimization AAPs (Alignment Activation Protocols™) as an on-demand, 24/7 healing system accessible via smartphone, tablet, or computer. These AAPs eliminate negative imprints that hinder your goals and dreams, often producing immediate results. Barbara provides this healing through a home-study course and offers one-on-one sessions for accelerated healing.

Barbara holds master certifications in the Yuen Method (Chinese Energy Medicine), Shambala Multi-Dimensional Healing, Reiki, and complementary and alternative medicine. Her work integrates advanced distant energy healing techniques with her unique Energy Optimization process and AAPs, honed over two decades.

With Barbara Robins, healing is fun, fast, and easy. Transform your relationship with healing today. Receive a complimentary 15-minute consultation by visiting barbarascalendar.com and booking a "Sessions - No Cost > Brief Consult".

For more information, go to: HealingIsFun.com.

If you enjoyed this Itty Bitty™ Book, you might also like ...

- Your Amazing Itty Bitty™ Relationships as a Spiritual Practice Book
  – Deborah Gayle
- Your Amazing Itty Bitty™ HR Challenges for all Business Owners Book
  – Amber Trail
- Your Amazing Itty Bitty™ Self-Esteem Book – Jade Elizabeth

Or any of the other Amazing Itty Bitty™ books available online at www.ittybittypublishing.com

www.ingramcontent.com/pod-product-compliance
Lightning Source LLC
Chambersburg PA
CBHW071412200326
41520CB00014B/3404